FORK
in the
ROAD

YOLANDA ROBINSON

Palmetto Publishing Group, LLC
Charleston, SC

Copyright © 2016 by Yolanda Robinson
All rights reserved. No portion of this book may be reproduced, stored in a retrieval system, or transmitted in any form by any means—electronic, mechanical, photocopy, recording, or other—except for brief quotations in printed reviews, without prior permission of the publisher.

For more information regarding special discounts for bulk purchases, please contact Palmetto Publishing Group at Info@PalmettoPublishingGroup.com.

ISBN-13: 978-1-944313-52-4
ISBN-10: 1-944313-52-4

Nana,

Thank you for letting me run my race.

Red,

You never stop believing.

chapter 1

How Did I Get Here?

How did I get here? I remember thinking as I was preparing for yet another jail stint. I had just finished doing eleven months and twenty-nine days at the county jail, and now I was facing another year in a work-release program.

Damn, it's almost over, I thought to myself, shaking my head. *Let me go in here and do what I need to do so I can get back home to my children.* At least I was going to a work-release center, but was that better than jail? *Yes, because I get to visit my children*, I told myself. *So yes, I guess so. But no matter what happens, I must stay clean.*

I remember Kevin, Yakesia, Devin, and Darius, my four children, holding on to my right forearm, and me saying to them, "Momma coming. Just hold on. I'm coming back for you."

They had already been through so much with me and had to deal with their own issues: having a crackhead for a momma, their daddy not being there, and all the peer pressure happening in between. The step I was taking had to be the turning point. I had reached my lowest point—losing my babies—but most of all, I had lost myself. I'd gotten to this point because I was hooked on crack, and now I was fighting my way back to my kids, my life, and my freedom.

You know, there's nothing special about me. I am just like any other woman who's had her share of life's ups and downs. There were many trials and tribulations in my life—not just dealing with addiction, but dealing with childhood issues as well. Those same issues tormented me and led me down the dangerous path I had chosen to take.

Oh yes, it was a choice. The first hit was free—but I didn't know how much of a price I would have to pay to stay high. The one thing I have today that I didn't have back then is courage—courage to tell the truth, the whole truth, and nothing but the truth.

You might be wondering, *Why now?* The answer to that question is simple: It's time! Time for true freedom. Time to take the risk to help someone else who's still hurting. Time to help those who are lost, who have reached a point of despair, and time to help those in need of a way to escape, who need to be reassured that there's a light at the end of the tunnel.

Here is my story.

chapter 2

The First Hit

"Big Dope, come on now. I know what you're doing," I remember saying, smelling what was coming out of the bathroom again.

He was smoking a primo—crack cocaine sprinkled on top of a cigarette. I knew mixing the two was bad because I had never smoked a cigarette, let alone drugs, but who cared? He got up and went to work, my kids loved him, and I knew that once he came out of that bathroom . . . it was *on*. Oh, he made me feel like a natural woman.

Sex had always been like a task, something for me to do, like I *had* to do it. Being raped at such an early age had really messed me up. Sex was what I did just to get what I wanted—but with him, on this stuff, it was different. There was a sense of freedom, the ability to let my mind and body go and just allow him to have his way with me. Looking back on things, sex had always been a real issue for me. When I found myself enjoying it with someone, I took full advantage of it, because I didn't know when I would get that feeling of enjoyment again. It felt good just wanting a man to touch me, let alone penetrate me.

Yeah, Big Dope was a man who could walk into a room full of people and everyone would stop and look. He was muscular, handsome, and smart both in the streets and with books. His clothes were always pressed to the point that his pants could stand up by themselves. He matched from his head to his toe and always smelled so damn good. He wasn't the type of guy I normally dated because he was from the streets. He sold drugs, but I trusted him. He worked; he played with my children; he cooked, cleaned, and helped the kids with their homework. Big Dope always made me feel so special because he listened to me and helped me; it wasn't just about sex. We both wanted good things in life, not just for ourselves but for the children as well. We had some good times together, and I really believed he was trying to do the right thing. I wanted to show him that I was the woman for him.

I was used to the nightlife. My aunts took me to the decent nightclubs we had in town, but when I was with him, we went to holes in the wall. Those clubs were exactly that: holes in the wall. Everything was going on in there, it was illegal but those clubs were jamming.

The music even sounded better, and a lady like me had no place there. I knew it was bad, but I was with Big Dope.

We would get to the club, and the music would be playing and it would be so smoky, but as soon as he hit the door, it was like time would stand still. People would just stop and stare. He was like the president in every spot we stepped in. His reputation as a "bad man" was true. Everyone always showed him love and respect, and if you got out of line, he was ready to do whatever to let you know not to "try him." I would hear the men whispering, "Who is that redbone?" I am very light-skinned and that's the word the men would use to refer to me. The women would be smiling because this hunk of a man just walked in. Yes, it was totally disrespectful toward me, but I didn't care because I knew he was my man and he was going home with me. I stuck out like a sore thumb, but it didn't matter—we were together.

That's all I wanted: a true man to call my own who would love me. I thought that's what I had with him, but when you don't have a clue what love really is, you find anything that resembles it and latch on to it.

He would put me at a table, get me something to drink, and I would be posted up like the first lady of the United States. You couldn't tell me nothing. He was "my" man. Yeah, I enjoyed the hype. The feeling of being important, free, and wanted. It didn't matter that I was doing things for the sake of love that I normally wouldn't do; I just thought maybe that was the life I needed to be living.

Man, that music sounded so good while sitting on that barstool. I couldn't hardly breathe because the smoke in the air was so thick. Little did I know, the traps where being set.

I stood at the bathroom door, quietly knocking, and said, "Let me in." It was like I was ashamed and anxious about the thought of getting high with him.

He opened the door slowly, looked at me, and dropped his head. From the look in his eyes, I could tell he didn't want me to see him like that. His eyes were wide open; he was sweating, fidgeting, and somewhat embarrassed. However, I could still see the good inside him. Plus, he was my man. I had him. He wouldn't let anything happen to me, and I wouldn't let anything happen to him either. We were in it together.

I slipped into the bathroom with him and asked, "Can I try it?"

I had been wanting to ask him for a couple of days but felt ashamed because I didn't know what would he think of me. Would he leave me? I never thought about how that one hit would change my life forever; the truth was, I just wanted to be closer to him. To be in his world. I thought maybe he would love me more and would never leave me or the kids.

∽

Growing up, I was an outcast because I was chubby freckle-faced girl, always subject to the fat jokes. Books became my best friend. I never allowed myself to become close with anyone, and I learned to fight. In school, the kids called me fat and freckle-faced, and it really hurt my feelings. There were some people who would talk to me when no one was around, but they wouldn't dare talk to me in public.

I learned early on that if you liked a boy, you let him feel on you, and then maybe he would like you back. I thought that was the only way I would ever have a boyfriend because no one ever wanted me. I remember hearing my uncle—the one who raped me—say so. I did whatever I could to try to shut up his voice in my head.

During class one day, it was time to eat, and as usual I could see everyone whispering and laughing at me. I didn't pay any attention to them because they did that all the time. After I got my food, all the other students blocked the empty seats because they didn't want the fat girl sitting next to them.

Okay, it isn't like this is the first time, I thought to myself. I was all too familiar with sitting alone at a table.

This particular day, a boy sat across the table from me, and he told me that I was so fat my mama didn't love me. All I can remember is going across that table and beating the hell out of him. I didn't stop until the dean came and forced me to get me off the boy. He stopped calling me names after that—everybody did, out loud, anyways. People didn't realize that my mama had left us and I was already fighting that shame and guilt. My sisters and I were being raised by my grandparents, and that was one thing I would never tolerate: anyone talking about my mama. She may not have loved me, but I loved her.

~

Before Big Dope, the few men I'd been involved with had all used and hurt me. If they lied, cheated, abused me emotionally or physically, I stayed. Being sexual with two women was just about any man's fantasy. So, the man I was with thought he was using *me*, but little did he know I was enjoying the fact that I could be with another woman. He ended up sleeping with other woman behind my back, she called and told me but it didn't stop our relationship, she and I were still seeing one another. These men capitalized on my insecurities. I was secure in the professional world but never in my personal life.

My childhood scars, though hidden, still haunted me during the night. I was still a scared li'l girl, but Big Dope was different. I felt safe, secure, and untouchable. I could get wrapped up in his massive arms and feel like nothing would ever hurt me again. He was someone who cared enough about me to help me—not hurt me. I desired love, and Big Dope was the man I knew I wanted to share my life with. It didn't matter to him that I didn't look like the typical "ideal" woman. He wasn't insulted that I was smart or that I was really striving to make something out of myself and my children. He accepted all of us. We were a family, and that was all that mattered. Yes, a *family*.

Big Dope rolled the joint and handed it to me. I was so nervous. I didn't even smoke cigarettes, and when I took the first hit, I began to choke. Almost immediately I noticed a tingling sensation running through my body. My eyes were closed, my body was relaxed, and I felt like I was in another world. I felt so good, so free, so liberated. And so sexy. *Oh, this is what sexy feels like?* I thought.

Big Dope and I finished smoking, and into the bedroom we went. He kissed me so passionately and made love to me like he never had before. It felt like we were sharing from our hearts words we could never express.

When it was over, and just before we fell asleep, he pulled me close to him and said, "Baby, don't do this with anyone else but me, okay?"

It was at that very moment that we both knew I had crossed a line that would change my life forever. Big Dope was asleep, but I lay there thinking about what I'd just done. *Do I stay or do I go?* The bills, the kids, not wanting to be alone, and wanting to get high were the reasons I came up with to rationalize and justify my decision to stay.

∽

The next day, life went on as usual. Our daily routine was to get the kids ready for school, get ready for work, get something fixed for dinner when we got home, and then start all over again the next day. Life wasn't that bad. We were actually doing pretty well. I had a good job, we had transportation, we weren't behind on bills, and my kids were happy. There was no reason to complain about anything—but my insides were screaming for more crack. How was I going to tell him I wanted to do it again?

Well, I thought, *I'll just have to wait until he's ready to do it, and then I can smoke with him.* But what could I say that would make him want to get high that night?

"Baby, you sure felt good last night. I wondered if we could get high so we can make love like that again?" I said to him after we'd gotten the kids to sleep. It was our time now.

Addiction is tricky. Some people don't get hooked after the first hit, but not me—I was hooked! I always had an addictive personality, and that coupled with my past and present issues. My mind was a battlefield. I was silently in search of freedom. That was all I needed. Crack was the straw that broke the camel's back.

Big Dope and I had started using even more crack, and it was beginning to affect us. Prior to the downfall, things had been going fair. We had our struggles, but we seemed to hang in there together, fighting to stay together and be a family. We were determined to defy the odds and make it. But smoking crack caused us to fail to pay our bills, resulting in disconnection and past-due notices. We were going down, and down fast. I was working night shifts by then, and he would get the kids off the school bus and I would be off to work. When I got home, we would get high until the early-morning hours. We were smoking a lot more by this time. It had only been 6 months and we knew it would just be a matter of time before we would hit bottom, again. Big Dope said we needed a change, so we decided to pack up and move from Pensacola to Bradenton so we could have a new beginning. *Interstate 75 south, here we come!*

We loaded up our minivan and went down south. My aunt was gracious enough to let us stay with her until we got on our feet. All we had was five hundred dollars, and that was going fast. We were both working, trying to make enough money to get back on our feet, but it wasn't coming fast enough. My aunt didn't mind us being there and told us to just take our time before we moved out to make sure we were both ready. We never discussed the real issues, but my aunt wasn't a fool, and the people in Warrington are known gossipers so I know they had told my Aunt what we were doing.

One night, Big Dope went to hang out with a couple of homeboys he'd met and came back with a bag full of crack cocaine. At first I was mad because I knew we only had two hundred dollars left, and how dare he take all we had and waste it on dope again. But Big Dope was a hustler, and one thing he knew was how to move product. So when the opportunity presented itself to make some money for us to get our own place, he took it and made me believe he could do it. And he did.

When he told me he had gotten a bag full of crack for a hundred dollars, I was shocked. We had enough to sell and—*yes*—smoke, too.

Big Dope could get high and still take care of business. I, on the other hand, was messing up. We had moved out on our own, and we were making just enough to get by. But it was getting bad, both the money and our addiction.

In one night, we'd gone through all the money we had, and we were going to lose everything. We couldn't pay the rent at our own apt—or anything else, for that matter—so I decided to leave him and never look back. I was mad as hell because we had made this move, and look at what was going on: We were no better off than we'd been in Pensacola. But the truth is, I was mad at myself because I'd allowed it to happen not just to me but to my kids as well. And I couldn't blame him for everything because it was my fault too. I packed up the kids' clothes and some family pictures, and I put it all in the trunk of our car. jumped in and my kids and I left. Big Dope knew I was taking the kids to their father's because I didn't want them to be subject to what was going on. Li'l Kevin and Kesia were old enough to know the truth; they saw the changes, not just with the household but with me, too.

As I was leaving, Big Dope said, "You aren't coming back, are you?"

THE FORK IN THE ROAD

I just got in the car and headed back to Pensacola. I'd told the kids they were going to be with their father for a little while, just until I got back on my feet. We were all very sad because this was the first time we would be separated from one another. But I knew it was for the best. He was their father, and I knew they would be better off with him. He could provide them with all the material things I couldn't, but he couldn't provide them with what all children naturally need: a father's love and support. His hatred for me outweighed any love he had for his children.

I dropped the kids off, and then once again I started rationalizing and justifying the reasons I should go back to Big Dope. The next thing I knew, I was back on the interstate, headed south.

Big Dope and I had to move to the projects to begin again. We made a pact with each other: No more dope! We wanted to do what was right and get our family back together. I wanted that, but the dope was calling me. It's funny to say that now, that it was "calling me," but it really did seem to call my name.

By that time, I was stealing from Big Dope's stash because I was tired of waiting on him, and I needed to get high. I ended up landing a very good job, but I would smoke crack while driving to work, and on my lunch breaks, I'd smoke crack. I didn't think it mattered, and I remember thinking, *Who am I hurting?* We were both working, the kids were fine, the bills were being paid, and everything was okay—so roll another joint. I had to have it. Things were spiraling out of control. Big Dope was holding it down, but I was the one messing it up, I couldn't stop getting high.

The kids' father called. "Yolanda, I'll be in Tampa to see his family," he said. "Come get the kids."

Come get the kids?! I knew I wasn't ready, but I also knew if anything would help me get back on track, it would be my kids. However, this would be a rude awakening for them, because we had lived in a home before they'd gone to their father's. They were now going to live in one of the roughest projects in the area. Hell, we were all out of our comfort zone.

The buildings in the projects were all yellow and concrete block. In the winter we froze, and in the summer we burned up. The kids each had their own room, though, so that was great. We all had to adjust to our new way of life because not only were the grown-ups around us rough, but the kids were rough, too. Regardless, Big Dope would get out there and play kickball with all the neighborhood kids. We were happy. Things were going well—or so it appeared to outside observers. I was still sneaking around, smoking crack, even though I'd told Big Dope I had stopped.

Good, the house is empty, I thought to myself one day. I went into my daughter's room where there was a big, open window so I could keep an eye out while I got high. I don't know how it was that I slipped, but Big Dope caught me smoking, and was he *mad*. He was like a raging bull. He put all my clothes in the tub because he caught me getting high, He put me in the living room chair and told me not to move, that I wasn't going anywhere. Lord, I was so scared, and I didn't move until he told me I could. I made it through the night without getting high, and I kept thinking to myself that I needed to stop, but I just couldn't.

My sister came down to visit us, and I was so happy to see her. My sister Baba and I had always been close and they'd always looked up to me, so I couldn't let them down. They couldn't know the truth.

When it was time for my sister to go back home, Big Dope left and returned back to Pensacola. *Damn, what do we do now?* I remember thinking. *Okay, girl, pull yourself together and take care of your business. Your kids need you.*

~

To maintain my home the best I could, I managed to not use as much crack as I had been. It was so darn hard, because I was still using and fighting to stay clean.

Big Dope didn't stay gone long. He came back home—having him back felt so good—and oddly enough we managed to pick up where we'd left off. That night I told him how sorry I was, that I would do better, and that he didn't have to worry about me getting high again.

Things were good. We were blessed with multiple cars and had money and prestige. My kids were happily enjoying the life he had provided them.

One night, we heard a sudden, loud knocking on our door. We looked at each other, wondering who it could be. We had just gotten the kids off to school, and we'd lain down to sleep. It was the police. Big Dope had an outstanding warrant, he was arrested and sent to prison.

I told myself I needed to get my shit together, but it just didn't happen that way. Big Dope ended up going to prison for something he'd done in the past, and it was like that opened Pandora's box for me. Little by little, the hinges started coming loose. I lost my job because I stopped going to it, and I lost the cars we had, too—even the 1976 fully loaded Cadillac Coupe DeVille. My kids loved that car. It felt like we were riding on air when we were in it, just cruising. Enjoying being together

"Is this Mrs. Peacock, owner of a 1976 Cadillac?" said the voice on the other end of the phone. "We have impounded your vehicle, which was used to commit drug offenses."

"What?!" I responded, trying to act surprised, knowing the whole time I had rented it out to a couple of young dealers in exchange for crack. I was then told where it had been impounded and what it would cost to get it out. *Damn, where am I going to get the money?* I thought. *Well, ain't nothing I can do about it tonight, so let me get back to what I was doing.* Yep, that's right. Getting high.

THE FORK IN THE ROAD

My firstborn son, Li'l Kevin, started taking on the role of man of the house. He was in middle school at the time, but he knew things had gotten way out of control.

Li'l Kevin had always been my little man, ever since he was three years old. I had been pregnant with my fourth child and in the bathroom crying after a brutal fight I'd had with his father. The kids' father and I had met up one night after I stole some weed from my mama's shoebox. After I had gotten high, I was crossing the street and never even realized a car was coming—it was him. He'd had to swerve from hitting me; it was crazy. Weed was never for me. Needless to say, a terrible fight had followed the incident.

Li'l Kevin had walked in the bathroom and said, "Don't cry, Mama. I'll take care of you." From that day on, he did just that. I feel like I took his childhood from him because he wasn't only concerned about me; he was just as concerned about his two sisters and brother.

The morning after that brutal fight, when it was time to go to his daycare—normally about a thirty-minute walk from where we lived—he wouldn't get in the stroller. He said, "No, Mama." That walk took about an hour, but he walked beside me and held my hand the whole time. He was three years old at the time, and he still holds my hand to this day.

My son and I grew up together. I was only fifteen years old when I had him—I was still in high school. I would drop him off at the neighborhood babysitter on my way to school and pick him up when I got off the bus. That li'l boy would not sleep at night, so his dad would come get us and take him for a ride just to get him to sleep. Everywhere I went, he was on my hip. My baby, finally someone who would love me.

~

Little did I know, Li'l Kevin knew all about the dope game. I tried to only smoke when the kids were outside playing or asleep, but anytime I could go take a hit, I would. I'd lost my job, so I didn't have any place to go. One day while looking out the window, getting high as usual, I saw Li'l Kevin selling dope to a man on a bike right in our backyard. I got so mad and thought, *What the hell does he think he's doing?* So I asked him. Kevin and I had always been open and honest and I didn't want my kids to ever think they couldn't talk to me. I wasn't prepared for his response: "Mama, we got to eat!" Eat, my son said.

Oh, I felt so bad, and then I found out what "drugs" he was actually selling! Bread. This boy had taken bread, cut it up to look just like crack, and sold it. I told him he was going to get hurt selling people that stuff. Those people worked hard for the money they'd used to pay him, and he couldn't do that. That was the crackhead in me talking then, but I *was* concerned for his safety. I knew I had to get better so my son wouldn't have to do stuff like that. I was ashamed of myself. But it didn't stop me. I was still using crack, allowing people to come to my house so we could smoke.

By this time, the weather had changed and I knew the kids didn't have heavy jackets even though it didn't get that cold, but by this time, Li'l Kevin had stolen some jackets for him and his brothers from the college down the street from our house. I tried to talk some sense into him, but there was nothing I could do because he had gotten in his mind that he had to take care of his family.

∼

"What can we do for you today?" the doctor asked me.

I was in the emergency room. I'd been having chest pains and couldn't stop coughing. I had all the kids with me because I didn't have anyone to watch them. After I told the doctor about my symptoms, he said, "Ma'am, whatever you're doing, you must stop, or you need to find another way to smoke it."

Well, since I couldn't smoke it in cigarettes anymore I had to use glass dick, what we called a stem. People used either a glass pipe or a metal pipe, which they then put Brillo and crack on, and I knew I couldn't do that. The stem was for people who were really bad off. *I know I get high a lot, but not enough for that pipe*, I thought to myself.

"Yes, sir. Thank you. Kids, come on. Let's go home."

I don't know who I thought I was fooling because by that time I had already been to jail for stealing money at work, and my neighbors had to watch my kids while I was in jail. We had nothing, and it wasn't getting any better. I was on the glass dick.

I knew what had to be done, so I made the call.

"Gram, please. I need to come home."

chapter 3

The Alley

THE ALLEY IS WHERE MY TWO SISTERS, Baba and Shamina, and I grew up. It was a dirt road with three family houses along it. The big house was where Madea and Grandpa lived. They had a red brick house, and there was a pigpen and chicken coop on their land. My great-grandparents were a pair of characters. Grandpa, whom we called "the wizard" because of his mysterious, gray eyes, drove a big, old, raggedy truck that he used to deliver pigs to different places in town.

We would be riding home on the school bus, and it seemed like every time we got to Warrington, traffic was backed up. Everyone on the school bus knew us very well, so they would holler out, "Pookie, it's your grandpa again!" I used to be so embarrassed, but after a while it was just part of our life.

Madea, she stayed home. She cooked, read her Bible, and raised hell. She was mean and did not mind telling you how she felt. She was also the church mother, so she was always preparing for communion. Growing up in church, we knew the importance of First Sunday and communion; it is the most sacred day of all the Sunday services. Everyone wore white and partook in what represented the Last Supper. We used to sneak and drink the Welch's grape juice. When First Sunday came around, those tablecloths were starched and white as snow. The whole house was quiet and Madea didn't allow us to play around then.

I can still hear her when she would sing "A Charge to Keep I Have" every morning before and after school. She would sit right by the front door in this old chair, and she would holler at us. For some strange reason, it always felt like I needed that routine just to begin my day.

The second house in the Alley was where my foxy aunt and my favorite cousin, Black Cat, lived. My cousins were all older than I was, so it was nice having them around. I always had someone to talk to, and my auntie's house was fun because there was always something going on. Black Cat and I would play jacks on the kitchen floor for hours. It was even more fun to spend the night over there. My auntie would tell us to go to bed, but she knew we would still be up laughing and playing. Black Cat and Tweetie Bird—those were our names. She was dark, and I was yellow. We had so much fun

THE FORK IN THE ROAD

together, playing out there in the dirt, playing hide-and-seek, climbing trees, and playing hopscotch. Yes, those were some good childhood memories.

The third house was where we lived with my grandmother, Bernice, and my grandfather, Joe Gillis. The house was small, and in the winter months, we were freezing, but in the summer we were burning up. We had one heater and used the oven to heat the house.

We had just as much dirt in the house as there was outside. That old carpet had so much dirt packed down inside of it, and Gram would have us sweep it. Saturday was our chore day, and then we would go get our hair pressed by Ms. Carriebell. Now, Ms. Carriebell was the beautician; she had a very small waist and big hips, and she could use that straighten comb so well. Our foreheads and neck would have so much grease on it that even after a bath, we'd still have grease on us.

Gram worked at a dry cleaner's, and Granddaddy Joe worked for a water company. Many days we rode in that water company truck all over Warrington. We used to go to the skating rink on Sunday evenings, and Daddy Joe would pull up, right in front of the rink, in his old Impala or in the water truck.

The Alley was our safe zone, and it was nothing but love. We were poorer than the other kids, but it didn't matter because we had love. We would play for hours—hopscotch, jump rope, dodgeball, foursquare—and when we saw that streetlight coming on, off running toward home we went. Gram didn't play with that staying-out-late-on-a-school-night mess. After a hard day's work, she would always cook us a hot dinner—unless it was Friday or Saturday, Gram called these days pot-luck, she would rest before preparing Sunday dinner.

Joe Gillis was funny. We got free water, yet Daddy Joe wouldn't let us fill up the bathtub with it because he said it would fill up the sewer tank soon, too. I still laugh when I think about it now.

Another memorable moment involving Joe Gillis: We were never allowed to change the channel. Our grandfather would fall asleep watching whatever channel and we would want to watch something else, so my li'l sister Mina would change the channel, thinking he was good and asleep, and he would wake up out of a dead sleep and say, "I was watching that." He and Mina would go round and round. She would make him so mad, and it would be so funny—but that television would stay on his channel.

My grandmother was as good as good can be. She didn't show much emotion unless you made her mad, but one thing I do know is that she loved us. There was nothing she wouldn't do for her grandchildren. She worked hard and prayed even harder. My favorite time was Sunday morning because she would get up early to fix our Sunday meal. You could smell the different aromas in the kitchen: ham, macaroni and cheese, collard greens, and cornbread. *Bobby Jones Gospel* would be on the TV, and she would have her church music on as she got ready. Oh, I couldn't wait to come home from church to eat some of her good ol' cooking. She loved God and her church family.

Gram had us in every auxiliary program they had: usher board, young adult choir, Sunday school, Bible study, Easter program, Christmas program, vacation bible school. If the church had it, we were there. I believe that's where my love for writing began—in church. I would hear things, and I would just write. It freed me. Our church's choirs were the best and everyone in our town—as well as others—requested us. Yes, we were that good. We marched down the aisle, singing from our hearts. My sister Baba and I were both in the choir. She stayed active in church as she grew up. When I got older, I started sneaking out and going across the street to be with my boyfriend.

Being in the Alley allowed us to be kids and enjoy our childhood as much as we could. Gram really wanted us to enjoy being children, and she protected us from much of the world's cruelty.

Grandpa would come to the house every Saturday and watch wrestling, and when it was in town, he would pack up me and Baba and take us downtown to watch real wrestling. Gram would give us enough money to buy popcorn and soda. We had to share it. Baba wasn't into wrestling like I was, so she would hold the popcorn while I jumped up and down for my favorite wrestlers. Back then they were Steve Armstrong and The Junkyard Dog.

But who could have known that even though the Alley at that time was the safest place for us, it was also where I experienced the most hurt. My uncles were perverts and anytime we were around them, their looks and touches made me uncomfortable. It was my uncle who told me that I had a pretty mouth and that he wanted to teach me what to do with it. My grandmother knew how lowdown and dirty they were; it wasn't a secret that we had some dirty men in our family. Incest was not unusual, and it had to stop. I decided I would protect my sisters at all costs, even if I had to play the role of victim to make sure it didn't ever happen to them.

My sisters and I were always together. My older cousin told me that Baba and I would walk from room to room, holding hands, and that we were always very close. There is a family picture of us outside, barefoot and dirty, standing next to Granddaddy Joe's car and holding hands. She was looking up at me in the picture like I was her hero.

Baba and I have the same father, and we didn't have anyone but ourselves before we came to the Alley. My mother later married my younger sister's father and we were exposed to a different kind of life. My mother was always smart and independent. I remember us having a decent life before she married Moses—that's what I call him because of his wisdom—but after she married him, I remember our lifestyle changing. We had nicer things, and Mama would have all three of us dress the same way. We didn't go to the Alley as much. Gram didn't have the money they had, but she would do the best she could either by hand-me-downs or from Great Day clothing store. One day, I remember Mama telling her that her girls didn't wear that stuff. My grandmother was so hurt, and it was then that I began to realize there were issues behind the scenes. My mother was always private, and when there were problems, she made sure her girls were protected from them. But as I began to get older, I knew something wasn't right.

Before Shamina came along, it was just Baba and me, so we would play outside in the dirt and act like we were cooking. We would get the leaves off the trees and cut them up like collard greens while we had whole conversations with each other. After Shamina was born, things changed because I then had an even younger baby sister. I had to learn to play with the both of them. This was a strain on us because Shamina couldn't really play with Baba and me. For one, she was too young, but she was also a crybaby—just spoiled rotten. But she was my baby. Now, don't get me wrong, I loved both my sisters, but I learned to be a mother by caring for Shamina. Mama made sure we all played together but she was treated differently. Everywhere we went, she had to go. Baba loved to sing, play dress-up, and do gymnastics; I was a tomboy, and my love for big dogs came at an early age. Moses had two dogs, Shandorah and Duke—a Doberman pinscher and German shepherd. It was while we where staying on the base that I was molested by the woman living with us, I was about 10 years old.

Before we had to move in with our grandmother, Shamina and I both had bicycles. Moses, our stepfather, put Shamina's bike seat on my bike, so everywhere I went, Shamina went, too. Baba and I—we were daredevils. There was this big hill that led to the naval base pool, and we would ride our bikes down it as fast as we could. Shamina would just laugh, not even realizing how much danger she was in. Baba would be right behind me. After Mama and Moses split up, things really begin to change, but we always had the Alley.

The Alley was home and anytime we needed a home, that was where we ran. Looking back on it all, it really didn't matter where we went because we were always Bobby Jean's (our mother) girls.

～

The kids were more excited about being home because they knew everything would be okay at that point. As for me, I wouldn't be alone any longer, trying to fight that monkey on my back. Gram knew what was going on, and it hurt her heart. Gram was a fixer. If there was a problem, she fixed it—but she didn't know how to fix *this* problem. Our grandmother knew the problems we had and she did her best to protect and guide us the best way she knew how. I don't care what we needed—she always found a way to make sure we had it. She didn't have much money, but she would make miracle happen on Thanksgiving and Christmas, and she made sure we had a dollar every day. I was always the trouble child, but she told me before she died that she knew I was a good girl. She told me she was proud of me because I had tried to stay clean. That meant so much to me because she knew before she passed that she had her granddaughter back.

I remember one night I wanted to use so badly that I couldn't sit still; my mouth was twitching, and it was like my insides kept screaming, "Crack!" I wanted to get high so badly that I could actually taste the dope in my mouth. I was determined to not get high that night, and Gram saw me walking back and forth in the room. I could tell she was nervous as she sat up.

"Baby, what's wrong? You want some of that stuff, don't you?" she said.

"Yes, Gram," I replied. "I'm trying, but it's so hard."

She lit a Pall Mall cigarette and stayed up with me until I finally fell asleep around three in the morning—and she had to be up at six to go to work. Lord, I had a good grandmother!

She prayed with me and got me through many nights. I was heavy into my addiction, living in crackhouses, and one night I had smoked so much dope that my heart was pounding. That didn't stop me, and I did what I always did: I put that piece of rock in the pipe, and off I went.

All I remember is sliding down the wall. I could

hear people around me saying things, but I couldn't make out the words. Then I heard my grandmother's voice say, "Get up, baby. Get up." I remember calling 911, and then everything went black. When I finally woke up, I was in the ER, and I knew that God had saved me. My grandmother and mama kept us involved in church, and God had been a part of our lives from early on—so I knew enough to know He didn't let me die for a reason.

After that, I stayed clean for a couple of days, and then—lo and behold!—I was back at it again. I was stealing so often that I had become really ashamed of myself. Stealing was something that had started way before the crack.

When I was in the fourth grade, my grandmother would always do her best to buy me the books I wanted from the school sale. The problem was that I wanted more than one book; I wanted them all. I knew my grandmother hid the church money in her closet, so I would go in there and get the money so I could have all the books I wanted. Reading and looking at different parts of the world through books have always excited me—so one book just wouldn't do.

By any means necessary, I found a way to use crack. Whatever it took. I was robbing drug dealers, renting out my sister's and brother's cars, stealing from my grandmother and my sister and the church, pawning my kid's bicycles. It didn't matter. I just wanted to get high.

THE FORK IN THE ROAD

"Gram," I said, "you need to get up and eat." Daddy Joe and I knew she had been sleeping all day, but we weren't sure if it was because she was tired or if something was wrong. Gram had been diagnosed with inoperable lung cancer, and it was getting worse. I called one of her close friends, who was a nurse, and told her Gram was breathing really hard and that she wasn't eating. Gram's friend told me to call the ambulance. Gram was dying, and I knew my life would never be the same after that night.

I was at the emergency room, waiting for the rest of the family to show up. Gram had on a breathing mask, and the doctor said that all they could do was make her comfortable. I didn't even know what "make her comfortable" meant. I was mad because my grandmother was strong and she didn't let anything get her down, and all they were going to do was make her comfortable?! Hell no!

"Do something!" I said.

Gram looked at me like she was saying, "No, baby. I'm tired. It's okay." She had spent most of her life working and taking care of not just her kids, but all of her grandchildren. She'd made sure we all had everything we needed.

I knew I shouldn't want to get high, but I needed a hit so badly at that moment that I went in her purse, took forty dollars, and walked to the crackhouse. I was numb. The dope didn't even help me, and my mind couldn't grasp what was happening, I kept thinking, *No,*

Gram. Not yet.

Then the phone rang. Baba told me she was gone. I just sat there, thinking about the good times we'd had with her—and even the bad ones. She didn't even get a chance to see me get myself fully back together. I am the oldest grandchild, and I was the one who needed her the most.

But that wouldn't be the night I stopped smoking crack.

My gram had been so oblivious to how the game went. I remember coming home and she told me that one of her church members saw me in the crackhouse at three in the morning and she was upset. I told her, "I know why I was in the crackhouse at three in the morning, but what you should be asking is what *he* was doing up there." I never tried to hide my addiction; hell, everyone knew about it—and why hide from people when I know God sees me? I kept going to the crackhouse but never saw that church member again.

What would we do? Our rock was gone, and she wasn't coming back. I had to fight now because I knew I didn't have a choice. I had support, my sister and my nana—and more importantly, I had my kids.

∼

Slowly but surely, things were beginning to look up for me. After a couple of months in jail, I thought I had made up my mind. "Peacock," I would hear the ladies call my name down the catwalk, "look outside." My sister Baba had brought my kids up there to say hello to me. Li'l Kevin would always "stack" using gang signs to tell his life story. I would reminisce about my kids. I would never forget jumping off that porch, ready to fight after I seen that boy hit my son in his face. He was being initiated into a gang. I would reminisce and just cry, cry cry. I wanted to be with my babies.

I had to fight like hell this time to stay off the pipe. My kids were excited because they had their momma back, and I was doing everything I could to stay clean. My sisters trusted me to babysit my nieces and nephews. I was rebuilding trust again with my family, and that was important—they all knew that the person I had become was not the real me. I was working again, and it felt good being the old me again.

One night down at the Alley, we had a house party out in the yard, playing spades, listening to the blues, and just having a good time. I remember laughing and really enjoying myself. It was income-tax time, so I had put away some money at my sister Shamina's house because I didn't want to mess things up, and I didn't trust myself. I didn't realize it at the time, but money was a trigger.

I wasn't even thinking about dope. I was enjoying my life again. Wouldn't you know it, though, my aunt showed up and asked if I would get in touch with my dealer friend. My aunt and I had smoked crack together, but she was more undercover about her smoking than I was. When things went wrong, she would just blame me, and then everybody would sweep it under the rug.

I called the dealer after she asked and he came over. This dealer would give me enough crack to spend the night with him. Yes, we had feelings for one another, but he said I didn't need to be out there like that. When he pulled up, she didn't go get the dope. He called me to the car and asked, "What's up?" I told him I was trying to stay clean and he said he was glad to hear that. He gave the dope to her, and off she went. We went in the house and she already had her stem with her. She hit that first piece and instead of me walking away, I stayed and thought, *Damn, here I go again.* The first hit, I tell you, is always free. When I hit that dope, that was it.

At the time I had a girlfriend; I had always had a crush on her, even as a little girl when she would come down our street dribbling her basketball. She wouldn't pay any attention to me, and it made me so mad back then, but when I got older and the opportunity presented itself, I made my feelings known to her and the rest was history.

I had a car at this point, so I went to pick her up. We went to a hotel room and smoked crack for hours. She was the sensible one, and she tried her best to tell me enough was enough, but it never worked. I was always like a beast, and until my appetite had been satiated, I could not stop. Crack is not whack; that stuff will make you kill yourself. I told her I was out of money, but I remembered that I still had some at my sister's apartment. I told my girl that I was heading out to get my money. She tried to stop me, but she knew that when my mind was made up, there was no stopping me. I wanted what I wanted, and I would get it by any means necessary.

When I got there, the door was locked, and I didn't have a key. *Damn, she locked me out.* She had a kitchen window right at the front entrance of the apartment. I broke that window and climbed through it. That was a hard climb, and I still don't know how I got my big ass through that window. I had to bust the windowpane with my fist and I had cut my hand bad, but it didn't stop me. I grabbed a paper towel, wrapped my hand up, got all my money, and walked out the front door.

There was a dealer staying at the hotel. He came up and gave us the dope we wanted; by this time, I'd had to wrap my hand up in a towel because I was bleeding so badly, but I kept right on smoking. I was on a three-day binge, just smoking, smoking, smoking. It was crazy. I wasn't getting any higher; I just couldn't stop.

You might be wondering why I'm sharing all of this with you. If things haven't gotten as bad for you as they were for me, keep using and—trust me—they will. Let me tell you something. The enterprise is real! When people say, "It's calling me"—it does. It's a demon like you have never dealt with before. You can play with it if you want to, but it will take you to places you ain't never seen before.

And it's not just crack; it could be people, places or things. Anything or anyone that takes you down a dark road of despair, loneliness, hopelessness, and self-destruction—leave it alone. Yes, I still made the bad decisions that have almost cost me my life. I'm still on the quest of love and married to a man who makes me feel good but who isn't good for me. Addiction is addiction, and yes, it takes on different forms.

~

It had gotten crazy. All the money was gone. I had lost my job and my car, I was living in a hotel room, and my life was out of control. I couldn't go back home, so I just continued to stay in the same room. It was a little studio apartment, so it had a kitchen, and by this time my boys were with me.

The girls were still with my sister Shamina. I didn't want to expose the girls to my lifestyle because I knew how dirty men could be, and I didn't want to risk something happening to them like what had happened to me. I thought they would have a better chance and more support by being with my sister—and that turned into a nightmare of its own. The one thing I prayed and fought not to happen, happened anyways. The cycle of abuse continued. I wasn't there to protect my baby. *Damn. Will this madness ever stop?*

Nana had paid for the room so we could have a place to stay, and this would be my motivation to try,

THE FORK IN THE ROAD

yet again, to get off the stuff. The boys were in school, and I had a very close friend who would bring us food to make sure the boys had something to eat. There wasn't much to do, but Li'l Kevin would always find something he and his little brother could do until it was bedtime. We stayed there for two weeks until Nana finally told me that she wouldn't pay for the room anymore and that I needed to get myself back together. Nana was always tougher on me than she was on the others. It wasn't because she loved me less; it was because she knew I was so much greater. Nana and I had a love-hate relationship. She wouldn't let me get away with anything and never allowed me to make excuses. It wasn't until a couple of years ago that she finally told me why she felt the way that she did about me. Nana was supposed to get me and my sister Baba and raise us as her own, but because her mom had told her not to, she didn't, and she always had false guilt about that. She told me that if she had gotten us, our lives would have been different.

The Alley was the place where my issues began to surface. As a child, the Alley was the place where I loved to be, but like I said, after Mom and Daddy split up, things began to change. The place I had loved I now hated because I just wanted to be with my mom again.

You see, I had issues way before the drugs. I didn't know what to do with all the emotions. I had no one to talk to about it. I had begun acting out as a child, stealing from my grandmother, fighting, and being disrespectful. I was hurting on the inside, and I had very low self-esteem. I didn't know if I was a girl or a boy—so I became both. Acting like a tomboy was my defense. I would have rather played with boys than girls because that made me tough, and I could protect myself. No one would hurt me again if I was tough—or so I thought. I felt alone, hurting inside, every day, and that just became the norm for my life.

Mama was there, and she did the very best she could by us. She was a great mom. She always put us first and made sure her girls had the very best. My mama had her own issues she needed to resolve, but she didn't want to risk affecting her three little girls.

The greatest love she showed us was to let us be raised in the Alley. That was the most selfless move my mother made. Back then I didn't understand it, but today I do.

I don't fault my mother anymore, but it actually took her having a massive heart attack and me not knowing if I would every see her again for my heart to be opened enough to forgive her. With that, the things of old just didn't matter anymore.

My mother was courageous—unlike me. I always thought the reason I had such a bad life was because of her, but the truth is that my life wasn't bad. My choices made my life bad, and because I was hyped up on pride, I lost my children for fear of being like my mother. I dragged my kids through hell and back trying to prove a point, and I was wrong.

The Alley wasn't so bad after all.

chapter 4

Tired

"Come on, boys. We have to go to the shelter, and they'll help us find a home so we can all be together again," I said, trying to sound hopeful. My boys were adventurous, and as long as they had each other, those two were great. Kevin was the leader of the pack, and Darius would follow his brother to hell and back. He didn't fear anything because he knew his big brother would protect him. He loved his sisters. Kevin and Kesia were close because they both had to grow up fast to help take care of the little ones and, yes, me too.

Kevin and Darius were still in school, so I had time to go search for jobs and a home, which I did do on some days. I was still sneaking to Warrington to get high, but I was getting tired. I knew there was a better way because I had lived it before. I had been to rehab, so I knew the steps. I had family and friends who believed in me, so I had a support system. *Let's try and make it work this time*, I thought to myself.

Lord knows I had done everything there was to think and do, so I was ready to stop. My kids needed me, and I was living in a shelter. *It doesn't get any worse than this*, I thought. After three weeks in a shelter, we finally had a place to stay. The place was in one of the worst projects in the area, but I was not going there to stay forever. This was a starting point.

"Wow," said all the kids. They were excited because this was the first time in six months we had all been together Yeah, there were times we'd had our own places, but due to my drug use, I kept messing things up.

Drugs had totally wrecked not just my life, but the lives of my family members as well. I was using so much that it took everything in my power to keep things afloat. I remember selling all my food stamps to the drug dealer, and he felt so bad that he called my son to give some of the stamps back so my kids could eat. I stole my sister's ATM card and took everything out of her account except nineteen dollars. She went to the bank when she noticed what had happened and she saw me on camera, but she didn't have the heart to press charges or ask me to give her back the money because of how bad I looked. She told me how much it broke her heart to see me like that.

I was binging three to four times a day. It was bad. After my grandmother died, I forged her refund check, and Yes, I even sold myself. We called it getting "tricked." Whatever I had to do, I did it. I just wanted crack. It had gotten that bad and would get even worse.

If you're using and haven't done any of these things yet, just keep using—you will. My addiction wasn't by choice. I was telling my story in a Narcotics Anonymous meeting. I knew I had to stay clean, and this time I was going to make it. This time would be different.

My girlfriend moved in with us. We were living as a family. I had entered an outpatient drug-counseling program and started staying clean one day at a time. I was going to NA meetings, and I got the best sponsor in that program. I began working on each of the "steps," and I made it to ninety days. I was working and doing well. The kids were happy, and then all of a sudden—bam! I was on the pipe again.

What happened? First of all, my sponsor told me about the acronym HALT (hungry, angry, lonely, tired), but I didn't take heed. When they said I needed to change my old friends and old hangouts, they meant just that—I needed to make these changes. I began to associate with people who were getting high, and I was no longer working honestly on the program. I figured after spending a little bit of time being clean, I could handle the drug in moderation—but it didn't take long before the vicious cycle started again.

I was back struggling with a full-blown addiction. My two oldest kids, Kevin and Kesia, knew what was happening, and they did everything they could to shield the younger children. I started getting high in the house. I sold my son's stereo while he was asleep, and all he asked for was the CD that had been inside in the system. The dealer would not give it back, however.

My dealer propositioned me with crack in exchange for my oldest daughter. I accepted. I smoked his dope, and when he went into the room for my daughter, I called the police. I had reached an all-time low. I decided to end my life. I cut my wrist and lay in the bed. My son Li'l Kevin came in, covered me up, and called for help. He said, "Mama, don't leave me like this."

After I tried to commit suicide, I ended up in the stress center for a week, but I had to go home—right back to the projects. I was so scared because I knew I couldn't stay clean living there, but I had nowhere else to go. I was all right for a couple of days, but by the time Thanksgiving rolled around, I was so high my daughter and my niece had to boil the turkey for Thanksgiving dinner. I slept right through it.

When was enough going to be *enough*?

chapter 5

Turning Point

IT WAS JUNE 19, 2001. I was sitting on Nana's floor thinking about the work-release center I had to go to in the morning. I had just come home from serving fourteen months in two county jails.

"When will all this be over, Nana, so I can get on with my life?" I asked her.

Nana gave me a stunned look in the loving way she always did and simply said, "Soon." That was easy for her to say. She wasn't the one who was going to jail for a year. I tried to get my mind off of things so I could enjoy the last day with my kids. It had been so long since I had been around my family. I didn't want it to end. Yet I felt like a stranger.

I told the kids to come help me pack. I was glad Nana was the kind of person who didn't throw things away. She always felt someone could use the clothes and shoes that were left at her home. She still had all of my things. *At least I'll be nicely dressed*, I thought. My baby sister Shamina had done my hair in goddess braids because she knew the only thing I was going to do to my hair was put it in a ponytail. That was my security.

The kids and I packed my suitcase, put it aside, and decided we would go to the park. My kids looked at me like I was crazy when I suggested we swing on the swings. They had gotten too big for that. Little did they know that it was for me.

When I was younger, I loved the swings. I would swing as high as I could, trying to reach the sky. It always made me feel free. My life made sense—no cares, no worries—just the open sky and me. My kids and I walked and played, and we laughed a lot.

On December 14, 1998, I lost custody of my children. Kevin was thirteen years old, Yakesia was twelve, Devin was eight, and Darius was seven. Kevin was with his father, and Nana was granted custody of the three younger children.

I finally called them over to me to explain to them that this was a work-release center and that it was the last thing I had to do before I could get them back. The state had taken them because I couldn't stay clean. My kids knew I loved them, and even though it was hard, they understood that this was something I had to do. I promised them that after all this was over, I would come back for them. They had been through so much in their lives. I knew I had to make all my wrongs right and I would be a good mother once again.

As my kids and I headed back to Nana's house, I noticed Darius running and jumping around. He was always a very energetic kid. He had come a long way. Pinky—my daughter Devin—always took her time doing anything. She was very independent. She was short and chunky. She took little baby steps when she walked, and she was always right behind me. Now Kesia, my oldest girl, was always right beside me. She and Li'l Kevin had really seen and felt the downfall of my addiction.

In the most sincere voice, Yakesia said to me, "Momma, you can do it." Those words were music to my ears. I knew my children still believed in me, and I knew I had to do this last little bit. With all I had, I knew deep down inside we were going to make it!

We got back to Nana's house, and she had cooked. We ate dinner as a family, but no one was talking very much, which made it feel strange. After dinner, Darius took a bath, and the girls and I cleaned up the kitchen. I tucked Darius into bed, and he gave me a kiss goodnight and told me he loved me. He still does to this day. I had to sleep with the girls, and their room was freezing—which was fine, because that meant we had to cuddle up really close to one another. I often wonder which of us was holding on tighter that night—them or me?

Kesia got up. I heard Nana say it was time for school. Kesia began to start her daily routine, just like she'd been doing the whole time I'd been gone. She didn't say a word to me, and I didn't say a word to her. I just went into the living room with Nana, who told me that I could drive Kesia to school. I smiled and told her thank you.

As we drove to Escambia High School, Kesia and I made small talk. I began to feel very guilty for having been gone so long only to have to leave again.

"Well, big girl, Momma will see you later. Love you," I said.

"Love you, too, Momma."

She got out of the car, and I began to cry. My baby, all grown up, still in school, and no babies. She was still surviving. I was very proud that she was holding on. I smiled and pulled the car away.

I made it back to Nana's, and it was time for Pinky and Darius to get up. Darius got up first, got everything ready, and waited to go. Pinky still hadn't moved. She finally came out and slowly began her daily routine. Pinky had slept until the last minute, but the two of them were finally ready to go.

I walked with them to the bus stop. I realized at that moment that I had never walked them to a bus stop before. We stood there, the two of them talking to each other as I looked around because I didn't know which way the bus came.

We finally saw the bus coming, and when it stopped to pick them up, I gave them both hugs and kisses and said I loved them. They got on, waved at me, and then started talking to their friends.

I stood there as the bus went down the street and thought, *It's my time now.* I felt so alone, though, and that moment felt just the same as the day they'd been taken away. I told myself I needed to get my stuff and head to the work-release center. I was ready to get it over with!

When I got home, I went inside and sat down. Nana smiled at me.

"Let's go," I said to her.

I had to go to the probation office before I went to the center. As I was doing the paperwork, I found out I wasn't allowed to have any contact with the person who'd been the victim of my crime. I had stolen Nana's checkbook and written $950 worth of checks. That was the reason I'd been sentenced to a year at the Pensacola Restitution Center. Nana and I looked at each other, and neither of us said a word. I had already violated my probation—and she was the victim.

Afterward, when we finally pulled up to the work-release center, I looked at the peach-colored building and sat there for a minute. I just sat there and sat there. I took a deep breath, and I finally opened the door.

Nana walked with me, and when we reached the entrance, I rang the doorbell. The damn building had a doorbell, and I thought, *What the hell?* Finally, a heavyset black woman came to the door, opened it, and said, "May I help you?" I told her my name, Yolanda Peacock, and that the Major Griffin was expecting me. She told us to come in, but when Nana and I started to step inside, she said, "No, only the inmate can come inside."

I turned to look at Nana. She was standing straight up. I could tell she was hurting, but she never said a word. I wanted to cry, but I didn't dare. Nana didn't like it when I cried. She always told me to suck it up, so I immediately did just that—without her having to say a word. We hugged each other, and I let go. I turned, walked inside, and heard the door close behind me. I wanted to say, "The hell with this!"—but I thought about my children and I knew I had to keep working.

We walked down a long hallway, and I kept a hard, cold look on my face to hide my true feelings. I noticed some doors open and then close as we passed, and it was quiet. My insides were a mess, and I was shaking, yet there was no expression on my face. We made it to an open area that had chairs, tables, a TV, vending machines, and two phones.

The lady finally spoke. She told me that she was the lieutenant and to put my stuff down and have a seat. I looked around and noticed there was a guy also sitting there. Who could have known that later on down the line, this man would be a driving force in helping me get better? I didn't pay him any attention that day. I didn't have time for small talk, and I hadn't come there to make friends or to meet a man. I wanted him to leave me alone. This was all business—no pleasure.

So what if the work-release center was coed? *Oh well*, I told myself. *I'm only here to do my time.* The fact

THE FORK IN THE ROAD

it was coed didn't matter. It was better than jail. The lieutenant began to ask me questions—my name, date of birth, social security number, if I had any tattoos—all that stuff. She said she needed the information to complete my Department of Corrections file. *Damn, this is for real.* I was DC #557053. Without getting too personal, I answered her questions. *Business*, I kept saying to myself.

I then had to have my picture taken, and they searched through my personal property. She assigned me a bed, and then I was given the rundown of all the dos and don'ts. Afterward, she took me to a locked door and turned the key, and when I looked inside I saw that the room had about eight bunk beds and a private bathroom. I immediately went to the bed in the corner, put my stuff away as I'd been told to do, and headed back to hear the rules. There would be no problems from me—hell, that's what had gotten me in trouble from the start.

This was a work-release program, and I had to work. I had to give them 85 percent of the income I earned to pay for room and board and fines, but I thought the fresh air and being around people again was a blessing. I would be eligible for weekend passes, too. I could go home.

I had to find a job. The center had an arrangement with Krispy Kreme, so I walked up there, applied for a job, and was hired. I worked from 11:00 a.m. to 7:00 p.m., which was perfect because it meant I didn't have time to deal with anyone at the center. I was the only female that worked the night shift.

Part of my court order was to attend substance abuse classes—and this was where the rest of my story began.

There was this guy sitting in the dayroom, and when I walked in, he looked at me like I was just another woman off the streets. I remember thinking, *Who the hell does he think he is?* And I knew I had to show him who I was. I had to attend substance abuse classes, would help me get to the root of all my problems. I also met a man who challenged me to be the smart, caring, loving, beautiful woman I'd once been, instead of the coldhearted girl I'd turned into because of my life in the streets. I needed validation, but the worst thing I could have done was to get involved in a relationship during my first year of recovery. Recovery teaches you that the first year is the most important to work on you and you alone. So a relationship would be another big mistake but this man had me intrigued about the possibility of being in a relationship.

Things would never be the same for me after I entered through the doors of the work-release center. Not only was I paying my debt to society and becoming a productive member, but most importantly, I was facing my fears and learning more about the disease of addiction. I was starting to dream again, to have hope, and to believe in the one person I had stopped loving and believing in—me. I wanted to live again, and it was

THE FORK IN THE ROAD

a very good feeling. Whether I felt at peace no longer depended on my circumstances. I didn't need crack cocaine anymore. I had come to a fork in the road.

Has it been easy? No. It's been a daily struggle—not because I have the urge to use, but because I have forgiven myself and have freed myself from feeling a sense of false guilt and shame. I have done some terrible things, and at times I find myself thinking, *What if I had never picked up the crack?* But I have to shake it off—and I have to shake it off quickly, too, because despair is part of the disease. Has it affected my children? Yes, very much so. Two of my children also struggle with drugs and alcohol. Another one is bipolar. And Kevin is currently serving a mandatory twenty-year prison sentence.

How do I know I will never pick up again? Two reasons.

The first is that on September 4, 2002, Kevin was sentenced to prison, and my parole officer was there. He saw how distraught I was, and I was two years into a three-year probation sentence at the time. Urinalysis was a part of my requirements, and yet he had enough trust in me that he didn't require me to take a test. Well, on that day I had to report, and he asked me for a urinalysis. I was livid. I said, "How dare you! Oh, you think I would use?" I pissed in the cup with the door open, waited for the results, and left. He later told me it was then that he knew I would be all right.

My parole officer was also a pastor, and I felt this

was God's way of letting me know that He was protecting me. Throughout my addiction, I had angels along the way who kept encouraging me. I now know that I can't be selfish when my son needs me the most. Getting high is not an option. I have to stay clean.

The second reason I know I will never pick up again is that I love the woman I am still becoming. God isn't through with me yet. I have been blessed with a decent job, I am responsible, and I have earned my respect back. I'm currently in school pursuing a doctorate degree in theology. I love the Word of God. His Word. His people.

I can't judge. My life experiences have made me a disciple because I didn't just learn the knowledge—I lived it. I have had my ups and downs along the way. Yes, I still cry over my past. It doesn't hurt, though. I only cry happy tears now, because I made it. I don't play around when it comes to my addiction because I know I'm still one hit away from becoming addicted again if I don't do the necessary things I have to do to make things work.

It's about choices. Right decisions. The outcome. Do I want to live or do I want to die? I chose to live, and you should, too. There is nothing too hard for God to handle, and if He did it for me, then He will surely do it for you. You are *never* alone. Thank you for letting me be myself.

About the Author

Yolanda Robinson, originally from Warrington, Florida, is the oldest of three sisters. She was brought up in the church, and she accepted Christ at an early age. She became a mother at age fifteen, and by the time she was twenty-two years old, she had four children—Kevin, Kesia, Devin, and Darius. Now married, she has fourteen grandchildren and a dog named Molly. She has been clean from crack cocaine for eighteen years. She also is the Co-Founder of Day4Day Outreach Ministry that supports both men and woman currently and formerly incarcerated.

Made in the USA
Columbia, SC
02 April 2025